EMPOWERED

A COLORING BOOK FOR TEENS

Creative Inspiration
to Build Self-Confidence

ROCKRIDGE PRESS

Interior and Cover Designer: Gabe Nansen
Art Producer: Hannah Dickerson
Editor: Julie Haverkate
Production Editor: Caroline Flanagan
Production Manager: Holly Haydash

Illustrations © 2022 Collaborate Agency
Patterns © SubwayParty/Creative Market

Paperback ISBN: 978-1-63878-585-9

R0

This Book Belongs to

_____

Attributions

Live the life of your dreams. —*Oprah Winfrey*

We young people are unstoppable.
—*Greta Thunberg*

I am not afraid of storms.
—*Louisa May Alcott,* Little Women

It is only with the heart that one can see rightly.
—*Antoine de Saint-Exupéry,* The Little Prince

Maybe everyone can live beyond what they're capable of.
—*Markus Zusak,* I Am the Messenger

Give your growth time. —*Lizzo*

Curiosity has its own reason for existing.
—*Albert Einstein*

Not knowing when the dawn will come,
I open every door. —*Emily Dickinson,* "Dawn"

I am no bird; and no net ensnares me.
—*Charlotte Brontë,* Jane Eyre

We're made of star stuff. —*Carl Sagan*

Peace begins with a smile. —*Mother Teresa*

Some infinities are bigger than other infinities.
—*John Green,* The Fault in Our Stars

If you don't like something, change it.
—*Maya Angelou*

You miss 100% of the shots you don't take.
—*Wayne Gretzky*

We dream to give ourselves hope.
—*Amy Tan,* The Hundred Secret Senses

Whatever you are, try to be a good one.
—*William Makepeace Thackeray*

Believing takes practice.
—*Madeleine L'Engle,* A Wrinkle in Time

Limits, like fears, are often just an illusion.
—*Michael Jordan*

There is nothing I would not do for those who are really my friends.
—*Jane Austen,* Northanger Abbey

Perfection simply doesn't exist.
—*Stephen Hawking*

We owe ourselves . . . the opportunity to explore. —*Neil deGrasse Tyson*

Be great in act, as you have been in thought.
—*William Shakespeare,* The Life and Death of King John

Your success will be determined by your own confidence and fortitude. —*Michelle Obama*

Two roads diverged in a wood, and I—I took the one less traveled by.
—*Robert Frost,* "The Road Not Taken"

Every child is an artist until he's told he's not an artist. —*John Lennon*

Any failures you have are actually learning moments. —*Phillipa Soo*

You are perfectly cast in your life . . . Go play.
—*Lin-Manuel Miranda*

You just can't beat the person who never gives up. —*Babe Ruth*

To a great mind, nothing is little.
—*Sir Arthur Conan Doyle,* Sherlock Holmes: A Study in Scarlet

Scared is what you're feeling . . . but brave is what you're doing.
—*Emma Donoghue,* Room

We are fundamentally good. —*Pema Chödrön*

Even a snail will eventually reach its destination.
—*Gail Tsukiyama,* The Street of a Thousand Blossoms

I am satisfied—I see, dance, laugh, sing . . .
—*Walt Whitman,* "Song of Myself"

Hope makes a good breakfast. Eat plenty of it.
—*Ian Fleming,* From Russia with Love

When the whole world is silent, even one voice becomes powerful.
—*Malala Yousafzai,* I Am Malala

Introduction

Welcome to your self-empowerment coloring book! The goal of this coloring book is to help you build confidence and celebrate your own unique style of creative expression. Coloring stimulates creativity, reduces stress and anxiety, promotes a sense of accomplishment, and encourages mindfulness. The great news is, all of these are building blocks to personal empowerment and higher self-esteem.

As you relax, clear your mind, and use your artistic instruments of choice, try to focus on the 35 inspirational quotes included in this book. These quotes have been chosen to inspire you to dream and explore—so be as creative as you like! Whether you've colored in the lines or gone wild, what's important is that you've taken the time to invest in yourself and complete something amazing.

There's no wrong way to use this book. With 35 illustrations ranging from simple to complex, there's a page for all occasions. Flip to an illustration that looks fun to you, and color in your new piece of wisdom. No two people will color the pages the same way, so use this opportunity to show off your one-of-a-kind personality. Keep the pages for yourself or share them with friends—it's up to you. Happy coloring!

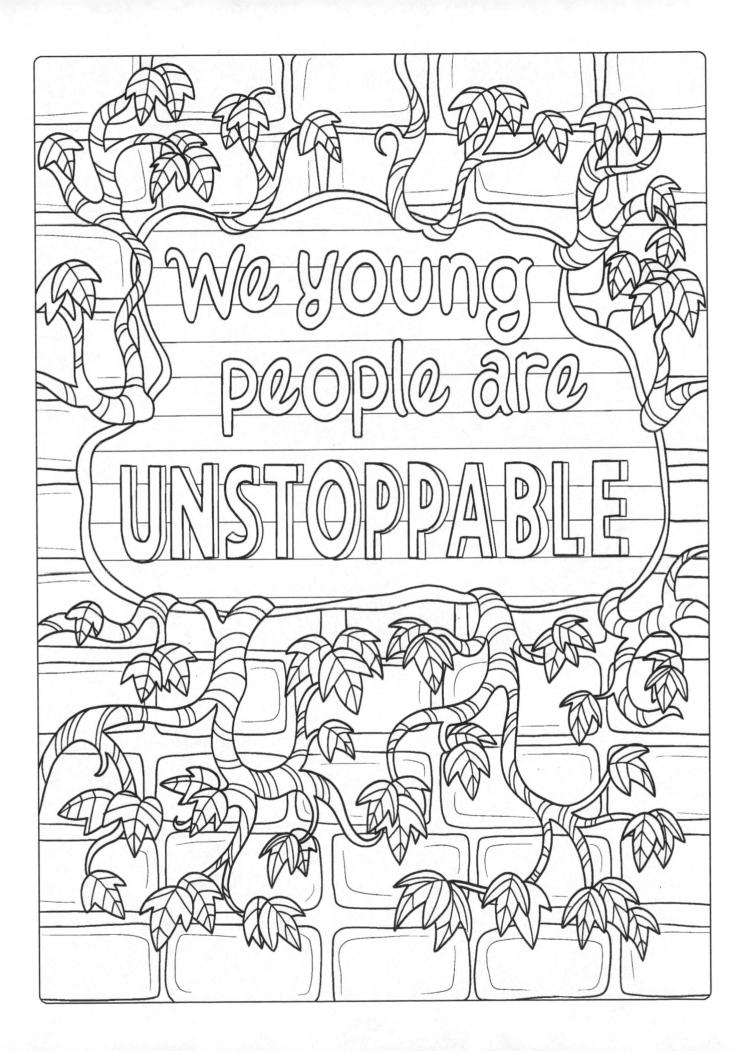

Scared is what you're feeling...
but BRAVE is what you're doing

CPSIA information can be obtained
at www.ICGtesting.com
Printed in the USA
JSHW030833020522
25308JS00001B/1